A WEALTH OF POVERTY

poems

john sweet

Contents

i. this is no way to live

the captain, the sinking ship

and we will do something or
                better yet
we will do nothing
and the lawns will all be green

the doors will be kicked in
and the children dragged
out into the streets

the votes recounted

zero for you and zero for
them and then none for me

the known

and then afternoon sunlight too
late to offer any warmth and then the
shadows of minor ghosts and
falling houses

the idea of hope
which gets harder to embrace

empty chairs in empty back yards

false visions

the death of the oldest child
which hasn't happened yet but
the image is unshakable

body curled up tightly in
some dark and filthy corner

the smell of ammonia

sound of a car door closing and
then a stranger's face
at the window

says he's brought luck but
his hands are
bloodstained and empty

that last summer

was further north
beneath the smothering glare
of pure sunlight

was next to you

was inside you
and had no more words

had no more beliefs

such an obvious
definition of freedom

on the road to the sun

no apologies for the
dream of severed hands

let the rooms fill with water and
the walls melt like cardboard

let the fields be buried
beneath piles of rotting corpses

tell your children this isn't the
future you wanted for them but
what did you ever do to stop it?

how many people do you have
to kill to stop the killing?

wait your whole tired life for
the punchline
but it never comes

the back yard, choked w/ weeds

we will only ever speak through
wires, through mesh, through
the tiny cracks in anonymous walls,
but don't let the future frighten
you because you'll be dead
before it ever arrives

you'll be history

     children
or no children

scars

stars

measure yourself with the words
of strangers, with their silences

let sparks fly from your hands

without god, there is only
the hope of brighter days

stranded

and lifetimes of hatred &
misery and oceans of dust

the man who calls himself your
father found cold and
hopeless on some winter floor

children born addicted

born healthy then
left for dead in hotel dumpsters and
it's a news story maybe but
not a part of any greater history

not a novel or a film or
a top 10 hit and not this poem
which is fine because
no one reads poetry anyway

no one dreams of the
ghost they will become although
it's the only future any of
of us has and so just
fake the words

just fake the emotion

just close your eyes and let that
pain pour out like a
never-ending ocean of blood

a lifetime

find a hole in the earth
big enough to hold
all of your lies

find the angels caught in trees
and on powerlines
in weak february sunlight

the low hum of distant planes

of electricity

i spent too many years in
this place thinking that there
were things that needed to be said

learned silence only after i'd
learned anger

found a hole in back yard
then started looking for
bones to fill it with

heard only the sound of
wise men ringing broken bells

menace

and there is always danger in
leaving a trail, in leaving proof
of your past lives

denial becomes an artform,
lies become oxygen

do you practice in front of mirrors?

on your children?

you are always more or
less than what you seem

[hope for you is not hope for me]

all of this man-made shit, the periods
                and eras, the centuries,
                the ages, and then you
        die in the end anyway, and then
        you're forgotten

buddha, christ, elvis, morrison -

fuck that noise

understand manson's way of thinking
and you understand everything

each day becomes a
failure of imagination

all gods are a reaction to fear

an attempt at self-importance

to be human is to be lost

to blindly chase wealth while
millions starve
is to be a self-made slave

there is no way to tell your own
story without admitting that
it has no greater meaning

poem from the final bitter sunfilled days

staring into the palm of the angel's other
hand finding only
     visions only
   questions only
   rumors of war

burying the bodies of politicians in the
age of assassination and i get tired of
                  every passing hour
filling up with the color of blood

i laugh at the violent deaths of
tyrants and mediocre celebrities

we are better than nothing
                and
     worse than most

Another way to hide.

Ring that broken bell
she said,
and she laughed,
and the sky began to cloud over

Thunder began to fill the
empty spaces

Distant,
like everything else out here,
but moving closer

to me you've become the setting sun

was like you'd smeared the sky w/ yr
opposite hand, streaks of grey and blurred
yellow, bruised silver, tattered blue and we
were mountains there and we were
continents drifting slowly apart on someone
else's map, characters in a pointless story
and the past was too heavy, the future
too bleak, too full of thorns and martyred
saints, empty rooms crowded w/ the
echoes of ghosts, the afterimage of
electricity, and it was always now but
it was never then and this is what i
couldn't make you understand

this is why i was afraid

all of the moments that i wanted to
remember were already in the past

...and all of us always in the shadow of picasso's castle

and in between the poems, monsters drawn in
pale crayon on the pages of this notebook, fanged and
smiling like benevolent cancers, smaller
creatures inside the bellies of the larger ones,
tusks & spiked tails and we've reached that stage of winter
where i'm convinced it will never end

i've come to that point where i
no longer answer the phone

no longer recognize my children or
acknowledge their love,
no longer dream,
no longer fall fully asleep or ever
completely wake up

do you see how grey becomes more
than just a color?

can you feel the damp frozen weight of every breath
that leaves your body?

all objects are poison in some small way

all fears are visualized,
            are made tangible, and
all silences filled in with sound

all open mouths filled with gravel and
                              broken glass
            and then forced to sing

forced to admit defeat in wars that
none of us ever even knew were being fought

bestiary

open the door to your father's ghost,
step past him into the wide open future,
no maps, no guides, and your hands shaking without
pause after three days sober

find the wilderness between ruined cities

dig your holes in some
blood-soaked january field

this is where you after a life spent talking
about nowhere, and this is the
animal you've become

find beauty in the lost just like you
take comfort in the found

watch the hawk fly up to the sun

listen to the laughter of the
man who shoots him down

vines, tangled with frost

no fear because you're pretty
sure it's a dream, this silence,
this late afternoon room with
the shadows of trees climbing
the walls, dust caught in sunlight,
child facedown on the bed you
sit at the foot of, your oldest
son, crying softly, dying, which
is a weight left unspoken, air
thick with the taste of metal,
of sweat, of the fear you
thought was missing, and you
can't get warm enough and
you have no words

you wake up lost
in an empty house

sound of ragged breathing

everything is wrong and it's all someone else's fault

a pale white sun in a silver sky and
all of the emptiness where
everything that hides
hides in plain sight

all of your father's despair and
all of his self-pity,
which is what he left you when he died

had a smile on his face when you
found the body, but that
might've just been the drugs

might've just been the simple joy
of floating up above the pain

[and that's the thought that counts]

wakes up that morning,
decides he's going to be the hanged man

makes it sound easy

makes it sound like
the only way out

six inches above the ground,
and not quite smiling

news of the massacre reaches the king in the seconds before his assassination

you in the center of
yr labyrinth on the hottest
day of the year

you
blinded but not blind,
mouth filled with the sour milk that
pours from your lovers
open wounds

you
without hope or
explanation

without purpose

feels so good, but at
some point you have to
start breathing again

beyond the kingdom of nil

and do you find joy in
the spilled blood of children?

yes, and i have
known you all my life

was a lamb
for too many years, but now
my fangs have grown in

now i am
the bringer of light

i am the prophet
of your death

of the days of hope
that will follow

the famine years

in the bleak grey silence of
early morning suicide in
the half-remembered dream i am
sitting at a window watching
                        snow fall

i am 500,000 miles away from
whatever it was
that mattered most

time
both backward and forward

i was there at his death and
i am here at your birth and it's not
the future that frightens me but
this never-ending present

so let us believe THE TRUTH
and let us understand that
it can never be anything more
than the most heartfelt lie

whatever can't be killed
becomes the
roots of the kingdom instead

you see?

space
both real and imagined

the 21st century grown out of
all the bleakest failures that
                    came before it

every single one of us a
half million lifetimes removed
from whatever simple joy we
thought we were owed

picabia's mask

crows in sunlight
    laughing

a desert of snow and then
    10,000 miles away
a desert of corpses

love of country like
a knife in the face

mouthful of ashes

cup of blood
to wash it down

nothing here but
good boys and girls

with nothing left to say, you keep talking

you in the
river of belief

you in the mirror

empty room in an empty
house at the end of november

addiction and conceit

gave the baby a name but
kept it to yourself

fed it handfuls of rust

fed it handfuls of
fire and whoever it was that
told you lying was easier was
telling you the truth

take a second just to
breathe then turn
towards the open door

run away from the man
who loves you most

crawl through the
purplegrey haze of
late december

there should be hope in every
act but this is not a prophecy

we were never meant to be
forgiven for the pain we cause

remember who it was that
gave you
this priceless gift

sunday poem, head filled w/ ghosts

don't apologize to
the dog on fire

don't hesitate to
eat its heart

to sing its song through
a mouthful of blood because
there is no message
waiting to be revealed

there is no true god but
the god of crows and
remember that the names of
your children need to be sacred
even after all meaning has
been beaten out of yours

remember that the dog is
born into hope

that the fire is set by hands
unwilling to accept the
weight of guilt

all choices
end here

like shards of glass, shining in the dying sunlight

left the bones out in the rain

had hoped

had questioned the
need for hope

man at the edge of the freeway
said *look* but then just
walked away

a child's shoe left there

an empty bottle of bleach

a frayed and dirty
length of rope

not everything is a clue

not every act
needs to be scrutinized

kept out of sight
though
just in case

Desire

Forget your fate, your fear of parasites, the
broken arms of winter. Remember the
simple holiness of being eighteen. A time
before the devouring began, before the
machine was built, was perfected, was made to
 run on pain and fear and human blood. Two
friends dead of cancer by thirty, another one a
suicide. A fourth was just standing there in the
store, was shot dead with a bag of chips in his
hand. Shot dead by a man who would end up
killing himself six hours later. Shot dead with
a girlfriend back home, a baby, and you never
really knew him, but he was eighteen too, was
immortal, and you need to remember this. You
need to escape the life you've built while you
can. You need to run.

the thought of leaving

book of poems found in the snow

vague ideas all melted together in the last
good heat of october and
shelly just wants to laugh and crawl

wants to learn how to beg

says *if words aren't the*
death of you it'll
just be some other goddamn pointless thing

self-portrait on the last morning

i am the reflection of
the sun in tinted glass

i am an unspoken apology

there are only so many
ways to state the
obvious

preliminary sketches

and bluegrey light without shadows and then
deeper into the forest

snow on leaves, on last year's bones

a still life

a landscape imagined

are you sorry you grew up
laughing at the truth?

the theoretician

hand in the lion's mouth and the
mouth filled with broken glass

this is no way to live but
your options have begun to run out

the fire has
consumed everything it could

picture a long empty hall leading
to a small empty room

doesn't need to be anywhere
you've ever been

picture sunlight

close your eyes

in this nation of thieves &
cowards you're no one special

in this nation of great failures
you could be anyone at all

poem after talking to my sister

14-year-old girl hangs herself
on a sunfilled afternoon, and will you be the
one to place the roses over her eyes?

will it be an honor?

an occasion for fear?

nothing is ever as
clear as i'd like it to be

pall

or the bravery
of indifference

of remaining motionless

of sinking

no one to blame but
the children who
no longer speak to you

no faith in archaic religions

the story is liquid

not eternal, but eternally shifting

the decision is made to
raze the concentration camps
& put up memorials instead, or
maybe shopping malls
or strip clubs

progress is
the important thing

ginsberg is dead and
burroughs doesn't care

the starving can be
fed oil & asphalt

vegetables from the
fields of chernobyl

i wanted to be a musician,
you see, but couldn't stand the
idea of having to learn
how to playan instrument

wanted to be an artist,
but had no original ideas,
no real talent

learned that poetry is
what you write when you
have nothing to say

ask bukowski

ask all the ones who
kiss his tired ass

the oceans keep changing
the shape of the land

prisons are a fact of life

you can scream and
you can weep and
nothing's going to change

j christ won't come
crawling back

stand perfectly still in the
middle of the burning house
and think about this

think about everything
you've ever bought because
you couldn't live without it

any situation can be
funny if you're
far enough removed

ii. a frame of bones: sketches & unproven theories

***

this picture i keep of you
from your other life,
when you were a lion

when you were beautiful

words and wisdom and a
taste for blood,
and when was it you died?

who was it you blamed?

***

in the photograph i
no longer have
you are smiling bright enough
to piss off every woman
i've loved since that
day

***

tell your sister she's bleeding,
but she doesn't believe you

tell your lover that each passing hour
just pushes the book of days
one page closer to the end

tell her all poems end in silence,
                    and then prove it

***

<pre>
you break the
baby you
throw it away you
              make
            another

              you
            meet
someone new
</pre>

***

and do you see how
happiness
will finally end?

will you come home
and tell me
you're ready?

***

a boy drowning in
a room filled with
people he knows

what you say is
he died alone

what you mean
is obvious

***

and the rich are
never on your side,
and you know this,
right?

you need to always
treat them
like the enemy

***

not afraid *of* my children
but *for* them

not afraid of the future
because i won't live to see it

you and i, we're as
good as dead by the end of this story,
                              you know

we're buried and
forgotten

***

in a room without
doors there is no need
for windows

in a room without oxygen
all you can think about
is the need to breathe

you might not find the
humor in this at first

***

you kiss me w/
a mouthful of light
and i'm lost

***

20 years of
punching a clock at the
suicide factory and what other
conclusion can you reach but that
all of the pain in the world is
someone else's fault?

what more proof do you need
than your own
suffocating misery?

***

dig your own grave,
then,
here at the end of august
and cover yourself
w/ birdsong

***

tells her his childhood was
just a childhood,
tells her his marriage was a
failure for all of the
usual reasons

discovers he has a talent
for making her cry

***

darker than it was
when we first met

and you said we shouldn't
and then you said we should

and then you came
like flowers in the rain

***

jacqueline calls to tell you
she'll be at the show,
then hangs up and shoots herself

the age of wild dogs
has begun

***

we can talk about bravery or
we can talk about poetry but
not both,
not together

you understand this
don't you?

***

let the weight of faith
be what
finally pulls you under

close your eyes as you
touch bottom then open
your mouth to sing

***

it's nothing to
admit you're afraid

it's cold sunlight
in an empty room

***

we should have been
braver or stronger,
should have been older or
                less in love

should have just kept
running towards
the late afternoon sun

***

bike in a ditch by the
side of an empty road,
one wheel pointed skyward,
            slowly spinning

this can only be the
beginning or the end

***

or this woman who says
that her daughter knew me

says she died in a
drunken car crash on the interstate
in the last hours of february

waits for me to remember

***

oldest boy says
don't stand so close to
the edge

says
i love you daddy

just like that

***

stands naked in a
february field, says
the drugs just make
her shiver

says his hands
always leave bruises
no matter how gently
he holds her

***

dead poet found in a
borrowed car in
a walmart parking lot

***

called up said yr
husband was gone said the
kids were asleep and
i was there in 15 minutes

i was back on
the road
before daybreak

seemed like we were
happy at the time

***

got there too late,
no one alive,
just the stench of burnt bodies

year zero
in the new world

best wishes
to all

iii. we mistake confession for apology

these days, wasted

like lions in the desert, she says,
but the truth is less obvious

find the point of entry,
and then name it

insects everywhere, and mold, and rot

roads paved and then cracked
and then paved again

doesn't signify anything, but it should,
and so you drive 200 miles in a
car with no shocks, no radio,
no windshield wipers,
and arrive just in time to clean up the
blood from the bathroom floor

you ask the child where his mother is,
and all he does is cry

and every true story ends with
the death of someone's dreams

flowers, early june

was a wounded bird, flew in through
an open window, and the girl there
was asleep but woke up in time to
realize the house was on fire

it was a small town in spain, which
means i've taken the truth and
twisted it into something more guarded

something more complicated

midnight, you see,
and the killer was coming

the children were dreaming

slow, gritty music playing quietly in
the background and i was upstairs with a
wrench and a screwdriver working
on the bathroom sink

we were all sick of the war

could no longer smell the smoke or
hear the screams of men
falling without hope

it was almost summer, and i was cold

was 39 and depressed and pissed off

couldn't figure out how i'd
ended up here, and
wanted someone to blame

had hands like the hands of christ

had visions

was trying to write a love poem
for a woman i knew, but the words
kept coming out like
garbled prayers dipped in blood

called her house
but her husband answered

said he knew who i was

told me exactly
how it would all end

laughed while i tried to
think of an excuse

the prophet, who foresaw none of this

the pale blue of lost afternoons,
                thin scrim of clouds,
                    uncertain shadows

not de chirico, but the
memory of de chirico

streets with names
that hold no memory

every house a faded grey and
not quite there and
is this the town you remember?

has the future always really been
just a place for the past to
come to an end?

i think i might finally be
ready for the truth

bankrupt

These small miracles of passing days, these
faded flags and broken windows, broken banisters,
sounds of children crying. Sound of the interstate.
Bloodline of passing trains, coal cars filled with
garbage, messages spray painted on the sides
in a language no one here speaks and the sun like
a losing fighter. Staggers, stumbles, casts pale blue
shadows over the dirty snow where hills spill down
to the river, fall into it, water reflecting
back the greyness of the sky, sky pulled tight over
everything you will ever know, over everything
you will ever be, and maybe it's nothing
to be ashamed of. Maybe it's nothing at all.

after the funeral, and then every day after that

say it, say
just like your father, and
let it be an insult

let your voice drip with
pure loathing, and why do we
always crawl downwards
whenever we're aiming
for the truth?

who taught me to see
humor in
everyone's pain?

and it's a gift, sure,
but i will be goddamned
if i'm going to act
grateful

[i am the ghost of years gone by]

gotta find that
sweet spot between
immobility and suicide

gotta breathe,
but slowly

let the dust settle

let the words
lose all meaning

it was going to
happen anyway

the frightened child, always

this january sunlight on december snow,
all dim blue sky and frozen clouds,
all washed-out colors like
memory or dream

you are here
despite everything

you are loved but seen only
through dust-streaked windows

distance is the key

i am never close enough to hold or i am
always pushing you away
and we mistake confession for apology

mistake solitude for escape and
the days are all filled with long lists of
gods who would like to see us dead

the air thick with the
memory of gasoline

of cold engines grinding
themselves into dust

such stunted minds,
such crippled dreams

so many hungry saviors
with the heads of crows

only the warmth of burning witches,
but it's better than no warmth at all

over/out

and i was dreaming about your death and
i knew it was a dream, knew you were alive,
and i woke up crying,
85 degrees at two in the morning,
empty house in a pointless town

had given up on escape but could still
appreciate the idea of disappearing

couldn't stop the roof from filling up with holes
or the birds from falling into empty streets

waited for the first grey light of morning

thought about the suicides of people i'd
loved and about the
bills i could no longer afford to pay

thought about my
children and had to smile

had to breathe and i was never going to
promise you safety because we were never going
to be in love and i remember that the first
lie tasted just like the last day of summer

i remember that the first kiss was
just as weightless as all the rest

how the world always ends

bones on a snow-covered roof and you
dream of reasons
but never the right ones

you wake up to
the screams of crows

stranger knows your name and
that your father is dead

a rumor of suicide

a child's body
pulled from the river

january now for most of your life and
all you want is to apologize

turns out hatred was
always the most important thing

what matters more than anything
about power is that
you will never have any

any vote you cast ends up being
a vote for war

there is never an end to the list of
people your government
tells you must die

all lifetimes collapsed into a single moment of doubt

you and i in the coldest room of
a dead man's house and
in january
this is all there is

five below zero at three in the afternoon and
who am i to
tell you that words are meaningless?

listen

we cannot be sorry for
every shade of grey

we will never cast shadows with
the lights out and the curtains drawn

and i will kiss the frost from yr flesh and
you will teach me the hidden names of
the tuatha de danann and in this
way we become holy

in the seconds before the
first shot of the massacre is fired
there is talk of a better future

it only lasts as long as it takes for
every child present to be slaughtered

st. labyrinth

you are chagall in his sleep
or you are de chirico in his young adulthood

1913, we'll say, and the winter
sun and the summer snow and when you
grow tired of remembering things that never
happened then it's time to die

and this was the guiding force of my
father's life but let's say you're
lee krasner in the winter of '57

let's say you're kay sage

there is always a horizon in the
indeterminate distance
and you will never reach it

it's 1955 and then it's 1959
and then it's 1963

pull the trigger

all pain and
no pain at all

the warning

was trying not to get
blood on the flag but there's always
some jerkoff who insists on getting
                        shot to death

a wrong turn or a plane
blowing up over the ocean and this
man holding his bagful of bones
says it's all for a cause

the children at the end of the hall
whisper *good night*

loss of hope and loss of sight and
assia dying just like
sylvia before her

kay finding a different path

tried calling dorothea to wish her
happy birthday
but she was still in mourning

max was still dead

had the strength
but not the cunning

heard god's fist pounding on the
closed door of an empty room

do you see how it might matter?

everything's brighter in my
dreams, but already fading

all of my speeches are
given by strangers

this woman who stands
knee deep in the flood says
the house is on fire and
this is the truth but i don't know
                          her name

have no use for anyone's pain but
my own now and
even this becomes tedious

born endlessly into a
nation of assholes with guns where
                          eventually
everything is said and all words
proven meaningless

all stolen moments are the ones
that matter most

girl on the railroad tracks tells you
this, smiles at the handful of
broken glass you hold out to her

and we are all the delicate
flight of sparrows

we are all
nothing but violence

run back home to yr
children and break the news

[i'll be satisfied not to read in between the lines]

thinking it might stop raining
but it never does

hoping the beer holds out for
another day or two

hoping j christ has a
better plan for the future,
or at least some money

at least an apartment we can
bring the girls to

it's such a goddamned
waste of time just
driving around in this car,
talking

the bleeding horse at the edge of the forest

ice in the river and the plastic bags in
tree branches and if you
call it silence
then you need to be prepared

if you drive north
the mountains begin to drift apart

the fields,
which understand fences

which understand the ease of being lost
with no hope of ever getting found

and the girl was eleven i think
when she disappeared
and this was fifteen years ago

my girlfriend was pregnant and
the road went nowhere

went past an empty house with a
starving dog chained to
a tree in the front yard and i
didn't stop

i considered how deep
the hole would need top be dug

how many times i'd have to
tell the story before it
lost all meaning

before it ended up being who i was

the fine art of finding a man who deserves to die

ghost town sunday afternoon in
the land of butchered natives

burnt hills and liquid heat
beneath copper skies

the victory of abandoned shopping malls
surrounded by weed-filled parking lots

the victory of
someone else's children
locked like animals in cages

let the winners
step forward and be shot

no harm

i am tired of writing letters to
the teenage suicide i used to be

i am tired of the
almost-sunlight

the sense of loss

who is it that builds a
town in nothing but shades of grey?

who is it that builds the workers' houses
in the poisoned shadows of factories?

consider democracy

consider nihilism

only one of them can
exist without the other

only a kingdom of fools would
believe in
their own infallibility

a milkwhite god

a manifest destiny

find the point where all of your
most deeply held lies converge
and place your headstone there

the alchemist, grasping for meaning

all days lost, all
minutes, all hours

tell her this and then
close the door,
or maybe say nothing

write it down instead,
black ink on a grey afternoon,
and then pull the trigger

wait for the
sound of laughter

what else have you
got but time?

vast fields beyond the kingdom walls

in the aftermath of the war,
any war really,
they stood there at the edge of the freeway,
three indians,
and we drove past with our pockets full of their children's'
bones,
with the sunlight hard against our eyes,
and the starving went unmentioned

the sky was blue, like time frozen and made holy,
and the trees had just begun to turn

it was that last year before the true famine,
when we still believed in miracles,
when we still knew the names of every saint

it was three indians on the side of the road,
and one of them blind,
and i couldn't make out the sign he held,
and then we were past

it was a dream about starving children devoured by wolves
and i couldn't speak

stood nailed to the railroad tracks,
sat frozen on the living room floor while the flames approached,
fell endlessly down some abandoned well,
and when i woke up the sun was in my eyes

we were moving fast past dead black water,
past the dead black trees that rose up leafless out of it

it was three tiny crosses on the side of the highway,
markers left by anonymous hands and
nothing in any direction for a hundred miles,
and it was a wreath of dying flowers

it was where the bodies had been found,
or maybe where they'd last been seen

the air was chalkwhite and dizzying,
hot,
thick with tar and gasoline

it was summer,
towards the end of the war

we were neither here nor there

song of the wounded horse

18-year-old girl naked &
beautiful in the room at the end of
the hall and will you be the one
to tell her that christ is dead?

don't just stand there
while the trailer begins to burn

don't think you can ever stop a
war being fought for profit

the sink in the bathroom drips and
the children are hungry and
i am tired of being told to take
pity on the junkies

i am tired

40 year old ghost on the other end
of the phone tells me *we had to*
dig for seven hours to find
our daughter's body and what can
you say to this?

the men out there die of AIDS
or they live forever

the women commit suicide

there is nothing you can build
from the bones of angels but
i collect them anyway and at night
if you're quiet you can hear the
noise this house makes as
it pulls itself apart

in the morning you can walk
through the rubble of your past

feels like being lost except
that all of the pain is familiar

one possibility in the unending wilderness

head filled with
october sunlight with the
dying buzz of bees and
the smell of gasoline

hands heavy with both
real and imagined distance

children lost in the forest or
locked in closets,
man found dead in the woods up
on burnt hill road

some sad goddamned story, but
i can never remember it

a book of poems left out in the
rain maybe, or a museum
burned to the ground

the worn-out tedious
fate of christ

heart filled with despair when
the realization of
mortality finally hit

the slow passage of time, and why it matters

stand 5 feet away from the
painting and what you see is the
future folding in on
itself

call your ex-wife to let her know but
she doesn't answer her phone
anymore

spent a lot of time telling you that
all of these screwed-up ideas that you
let blossom into religions never
really meant anything and it
turns out she was right

turns out there was enough
pain to go around
all along

and we are not liars, but this isn't the truth

don't be the hopeless man

don't smile like christ when
the first spike is driven home

this is different, is meant to be beautiful,
a nation of whores, yes, but also
a place to hide in it

a house on the verge of falling down

not the poem but the poet and
the poetry lover and
one of them dead and one of them stoned

one of us caught in the
path of oncoming traffic

not a great nation, obviously, and
not even the promise of it,
but listen

your mother's going to die of cancer
no matter what

your oldest son runs away,
your youngest just disappears

the war continues
despite the false king's promise

children and babies slaughtered in
the name of gold, and then whatever elected
vultures line up to rape the corpses, and
can you come out of this clean?

of course not

we are all blind,
we are all broken, but
i remember being in love

i remember walking through fire

listening to *the killing moon* all night long
and i understood it

i became it

a simple metamorphosis into
transient beauty,
but then i grew up

then i was the hopeless man

looked in the mirror some
burned-out february morning and
saw i was no longer needed

saw i was
the end of the story

an echo

the age of liars, if that helps

a man who would butcher parents
just to pose for pictures with the orphans
                                    he's created

no love and so
no love lost

no future but the one the
scientists have been warning us about

this idea of overdosed junkies as
                    satisfied customers

politicians as syphilitic whores

you spend your whole life running away
and you still end up nowhere

you kill all of your enemies
but more arrive
and this is how
the past becomes the future

these are the words you need to hear
once it's too late for them to matter

what use did we ever really have
for the truth anyway?

we fall/we fall apart

he is standing in the
dead man's room,

windows closed,

shades pulled,

just a floor lamp with
a 40 watt bulb

just the smell of despair

smell of decay

weight of
unspoken words
keeping him nailed
to the floor

we keep talking about the future like we're going to love to see it

and this is the dead man's room,
but no one knows it yet

this is the clock,
which is has been known to lie

this is the mirror, which will
teach you to hate yourself

which tells only the truth, and so
maybe turn it to the wall

maybe smash it and feed
the pieces to your enemies

to your children

toughen them up for the world
they're going to inherit

song for a good dog

and nothing to do
finally
but set the house on fire

soak a pile of clothes
with gasoline on
the living room floor,
light a match and then
out the door

wait for the future to
figure out how
the story's
going to end

and i could believe all of your most holy truths

and this is not walking blindly and
we are not yet to the edge of the map

we are hungry, yes,
but not yet starving

almost to the point of bleeding,
and do you agree that
love should count for something?

have we set fire yet to
everything that will burn?

i have spent my entire life
knowing that
we are almost out of time

good luck

and did you really
spend yr whole life
getting here?

and do you
see why
it's funny?

a thing of love & beauty

the humor of duct tape holding
the corners of your house together

the false hope of summer

just takes one good storm to make
your mouth fill with bitter blood

just takes the election of one more
wealthy motherfucker to make you
realize the failure of democracy

the poor hold no power and the
weak have no dignity and
why would you ever care about
overthrowing any government but
                              your own?

why would you expect compassion
from someone willing to sacrifice
you and your children in a war
good for nothing more than
the creation of profit?

how long until you start
finding ways to get rid of the
                    real enemy?

the prophet's suicide, unforetold

in the half-light of these
hopeless november afternoons we are
approaching lost

no maps and no true
gift of clairvoyance

a rusted gate where the road ends?

yes

a garden of emptiness

thin layer of frost on yr
lover's lips when you kiss, and always
rain turning to snow as it moves
down from the lakes

always the severed hands of christ
left on your doorstop

a gift or a warning,
a message written in blood that
can never be interpreted

winter,
and then winter again

clocks that refuse to keep time

broken toys in any number of
bitter back yards

we will live to see all the
beauty we've created
replaced by fear